Three's A Crowd

These trios can be performed with any other combination of instruments within Book 2.

Flute

T0045182

A mix and match collection of 19 trio arrangements by James Power.

CHESTER MUSIC

Contents

Published by
Chester Music

Hal Leonard,
7777 West Bluemound Road, Milwaukee, WI 53213
Email: info@halleonard.com

Hal Leonard Europe Limited,
42 Wigmore Street Maryleborne, London, WIU 2 RY
Email: info@halleonardeurope.com

Hal Leonard Australia Pty. Ltd.
4 Lentara Court Cheltenham, Victoria, 9132 Australia
Email: info@halleonard.com.au

Order No. PM189521R
ISBN 0-7119-9376-9
This book © Copyright 2003 Chester Music

The instruments featured on the cover were provided by
Macari's Musical Instruments, London.
Models provided by Truly Scrumptious and Norrie Carr.
Photography by George Taylor.
Printed in the EU.
www.halleonard.com

Greensleeves

Traditional English

Grandfather's Clock

Traditional

The Entertainer

Scott Joplin (1868-1917)

The Yellow Rose Of Texas

Traditional American

Für Elise

Ludwig van Beethoven (1770-1827)

10

Allegro

Wolfgang Amadeus Mozart (1756-1791)

11

The Big Brass Band

James Power

A French Frolic

Traditional

14

O Come All Ye Faithful

Traditional Christmas Song

Ding Dong Merrily On High

Traditional Christmas Song

Ecossaise

Ludwig van Beethoven (1770-1827)

Buffalo Gals

Traditional American

Rag Doll

James Power

Bill Bailey

Traditional American

Traditional Tunes Of Scotland

Traditional

Radetsky March

Johann Strauss I (1804-1849)

27

Minuet

Wolfgang Amadeus Mozart (1756-1791)

Dance Of The Little Swans

Pyotr Ilyich Tchaikovsky (1840-1893)

Pyramids

Timing and tuning exercise